CHERUBIM

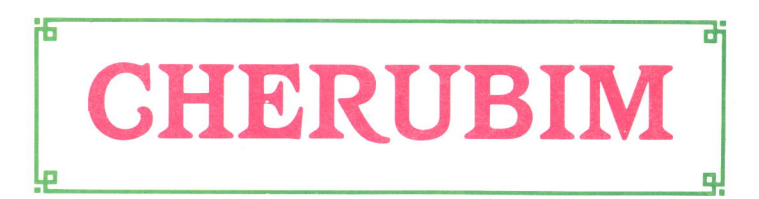

Story and Pictures
by
DOLLY BIEHL EVANS

ST. PAUL EDITIONS

With Ecclesiastical Approval

ISBN 0-8198-1436-9

Copyright © 1983, by the Daughters of St. Paul

Printed in the U.S.A., by the Daughters of St. Paul
50 St. Paul's Ave., Boston, MA 02130

The Daughters of St. Paul are an international congregation of religious women serving the Church with the communications media.

For my husband
Tom
my children
Tom, Wendy, Jill and Pam
and in memory of my parents
Marion and Edward Biehl
with all my love.

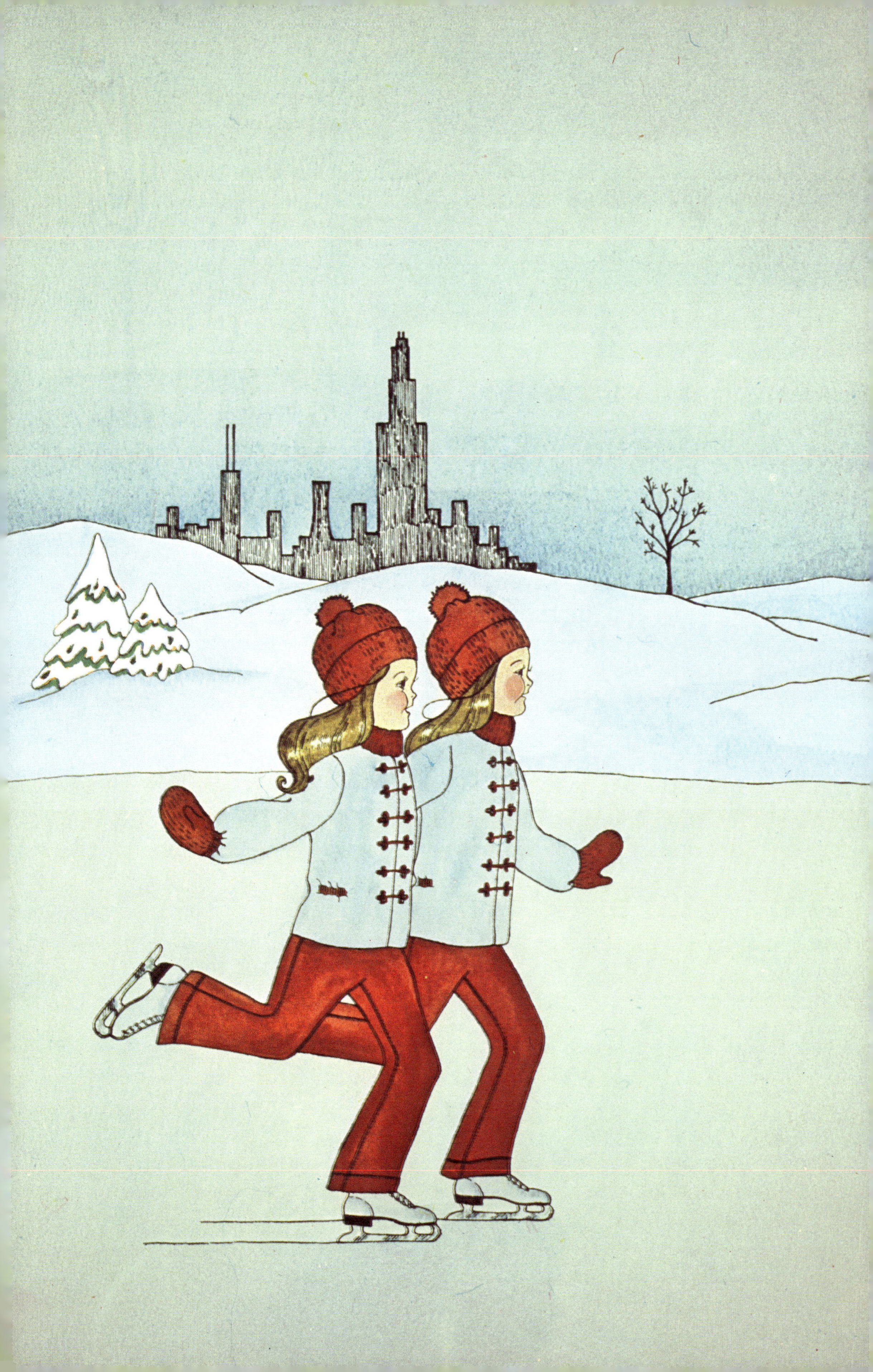

It was just two weeks before Christmas and some of the houses in Chicago were already decorated with holly wreaths and twinkling lights.

The icy wind swirled lacy snowflakes about the eleven-year-old twins, Wendy and Whitney Wellington, as they raced one another home from an afternoon of ice-skating.

They could hardly wait for night to come, for tonight they would help to put up their Christmas tree!

The twins were breathless and cold as they pushed open the door and rushed into the kitchen. They were greeted with the merry singing of the teakettle and the heavenly aroma of freshly baked cookies, as Molly Murphy, the Irish housekeeper, was busily doing her Christmas baking.

"Hello, dear children," called Molly. "I have some tea and cookies for you," she said, as she poured some piping-hot water into a bright yellow teapot and popped in two tea bags.

Spot, their lively Dalmatian, who had been napping by the oven, rushed over to greet them. The twins returned his welcome with hugs and squeezes, and he looked up at them with his large kind eyes, loving every minute of the fuss they were making over him.

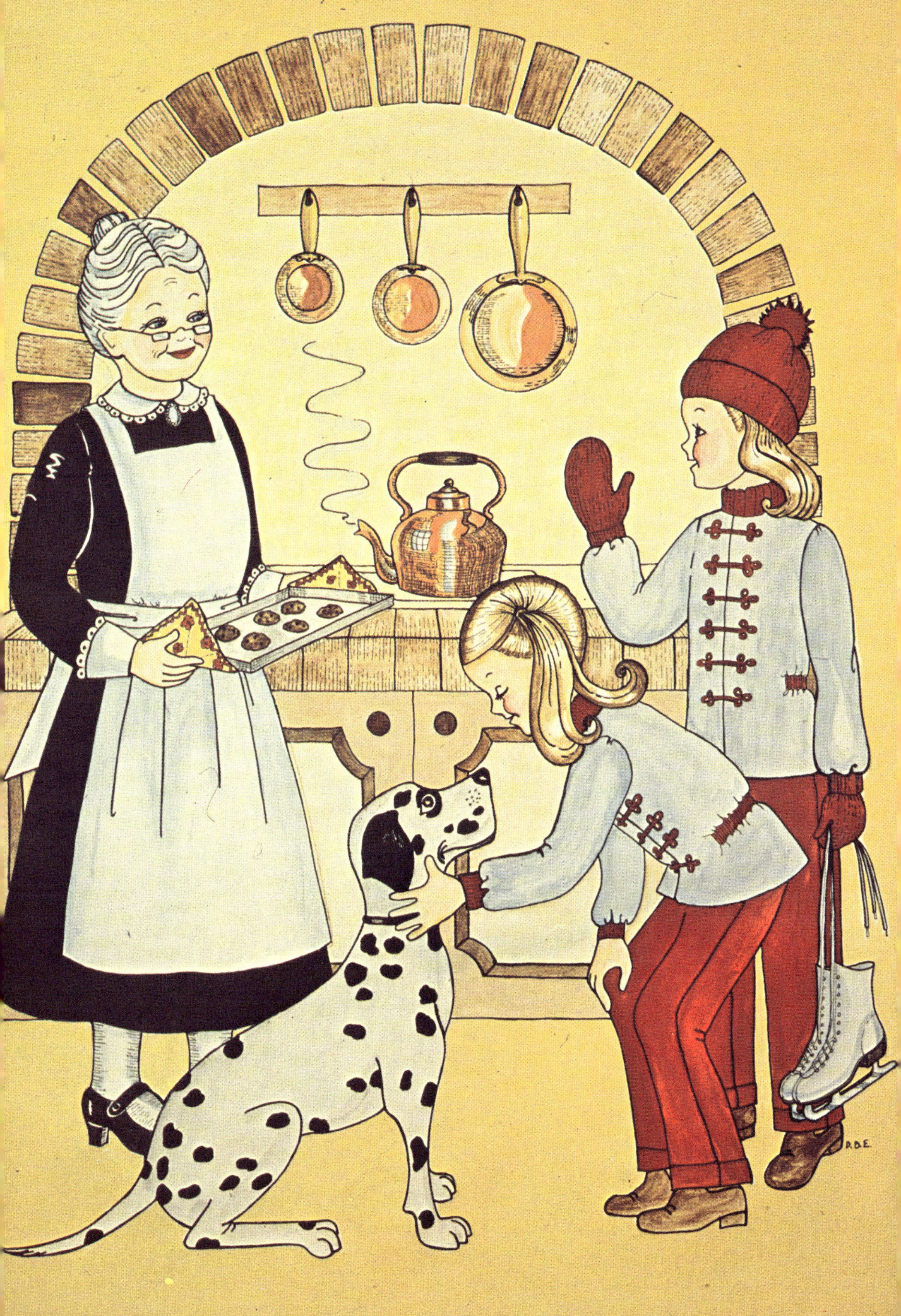
D.B.E.

After the twins had pulled off their jackets and caps, Wendy exclaimed that she had a brilliant idea and took two pencils and a tablet of paper from the drawer.

"Let's make out our Christmas lists while we are having our tea and cookies," she said, her eyes widening as she spoke.

"Great idea," agreed Whitney, as she hungrily munched on one of Molly's superb chocolate cookies. "I want a fluffy pink sweater, and a pearl necklace, a pair of western boots and a new record album."

Wendy thought for a moment and announced hopefully, "I want a new lace party dress, trimmed with satin bows, a new pair of jeans, an Izod shirt and a new tennis racket!"

"Those lists are getting mighty long!" suggested Molly, as she stirred the beef stew she was making for dinner. "They are almost as long as my Christmas chore list! I have so many chores to finish before Christmas: I have floors to scrub and polish to a high luster, windows to shine till they sparkle, and all the best silver to polish till it gleams. Goodness gracious! I'll never finish on time!" she groaned.

"Oh, yes, you will! You always do!" chorused the twins confidently. And they busily continued writing their long, long lists!

But what the twins didn't realize was that Molly was growing older each year, and when older people grow even older, they become slower and work becomes harder for them to do... and they could use some help!

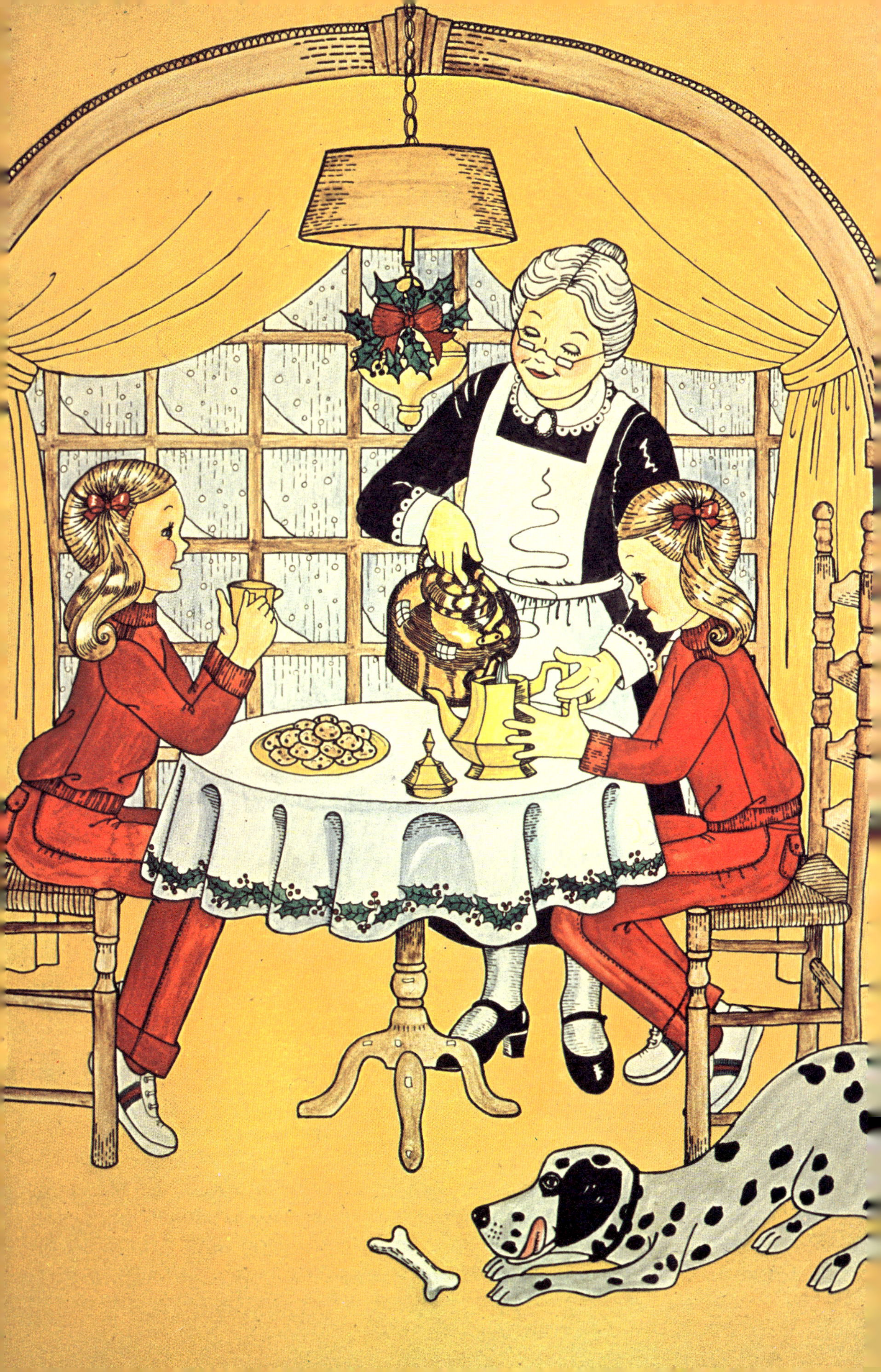

That evening, happy and excited chatter filled the kitchen, as the Wellington family dined on Molly's fine Irish stew.

When they finished dinner, Dr. Wellington announced that he was ready to carry in the Christmas tree.

He carried the huge evergreen into the living room and stood it in front of the window. It was so tall it almost touched the ceiling! Some snow still sparkled and glistened on its branches and its delicious fragrance filled the room.

Mrs. Wellington suggested that everyone help her carry the many boxes of Christmas decorations and ornaments down from the attic.

"We'll need lots of help, so you come too, Penny and Patrick," she called to the five-year-old twins.

They all carried dozens of cartons and boxes down from the attic and set them in the living room near the tree.

Penny carried down the very tall Nutcracker and stood him on the mantel, from which he could watch over all the Christmas festivities.

The very first box they opened contained the Christmas Crèche. Each year the children would set up the Crèche before they began trimming the tree. They lovingly placed the figures of Mary, Joseph and the Baby Jesus inside the stable, and Wendy hung the Star of Bethlehem on the roof.

Then the entire Wellington family gathered around the Crèche and sang their favorite Christmas carol, *Angels We Have Heard on High,* as Mrs. Wellington accompanied them on the grand piano.

ANGELS WE HAVE HEARD ON HIGH

Angels we have heard on high,
Sweetly singing o'er the plains;
And the mountains in reply
Echoing their joyous strains.
Gloria in excelsis Deo,
Gloria in excelsis Deo.

Shepherds, why this jubilee?
Why your joyous strains prolong?
What the gladsome tiding be
Which inspire your heav'nly song?
Gloria in excelsis Deo,
Gloria in excelsis Deo.

Come to Bethlehem and see
Him whose birth the angels sing;
Come, adore on bended knee,
Christ, the Lord, our newborn King.
Gloria in excelsis Deo,
Gloria in excelsis Deo.

"That's my very favorite Christmas carol," exclaimed Wendy. "What a beautiful way to start celebrating Christmas!"

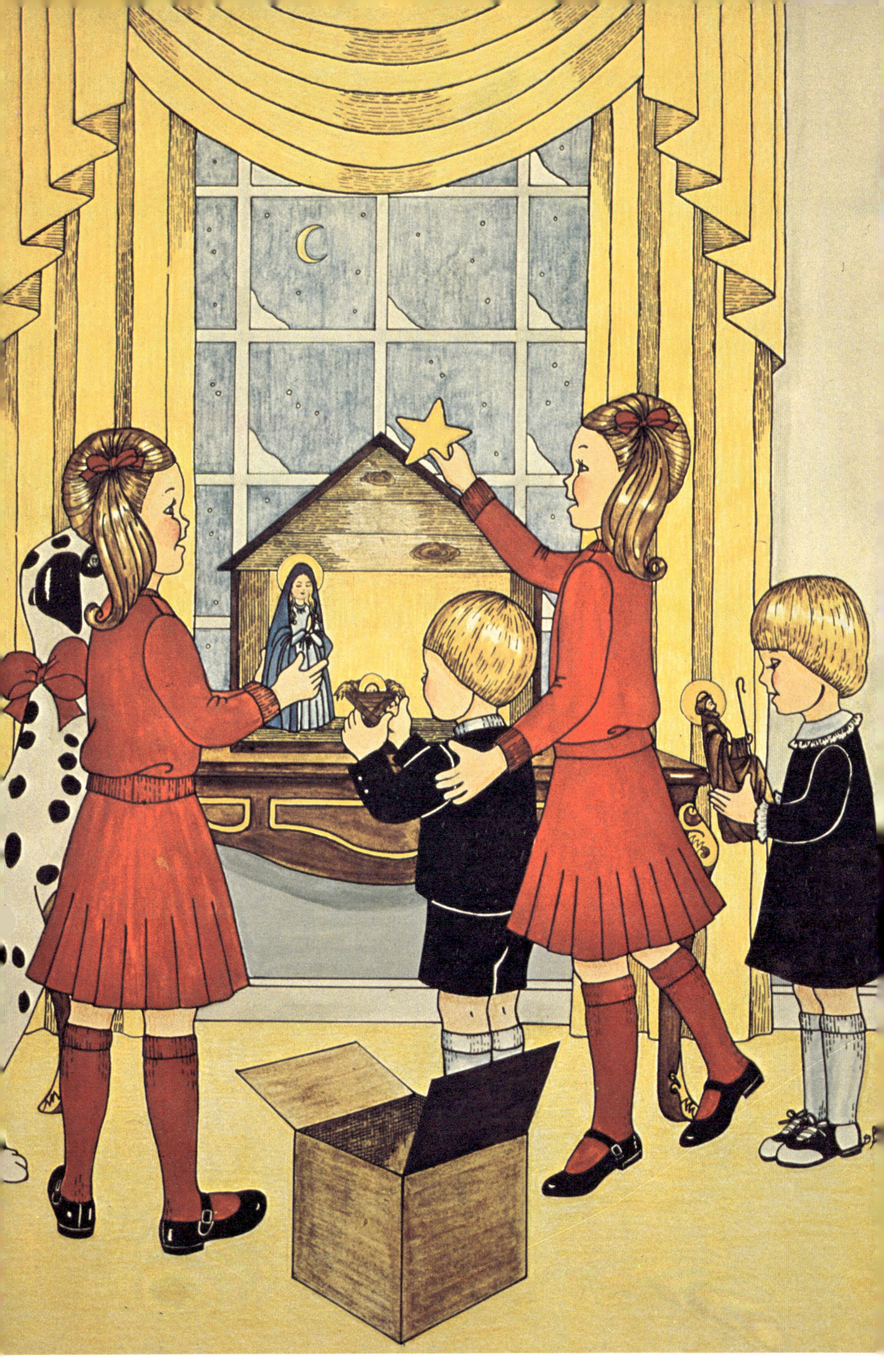

Then it was time for the party. It was a custom in the Wellington family to have a party while trimming the tree. Mrs. Wellington emerged from the kitchen carrying the big silver punch bowl brimming over with frothy eggnog and topped with mounds of whipped cream. Her pretty face beamed with happiness to hear the children's squeals of delight at the sight of all the goodies which she and Molly had prepared for them.

There were brownies, and cookies in assorted shapes of Santas, angels and Christmas trees, iced with bright-colored frostings.

What a gala party it was with everyone laughing and talking at once!

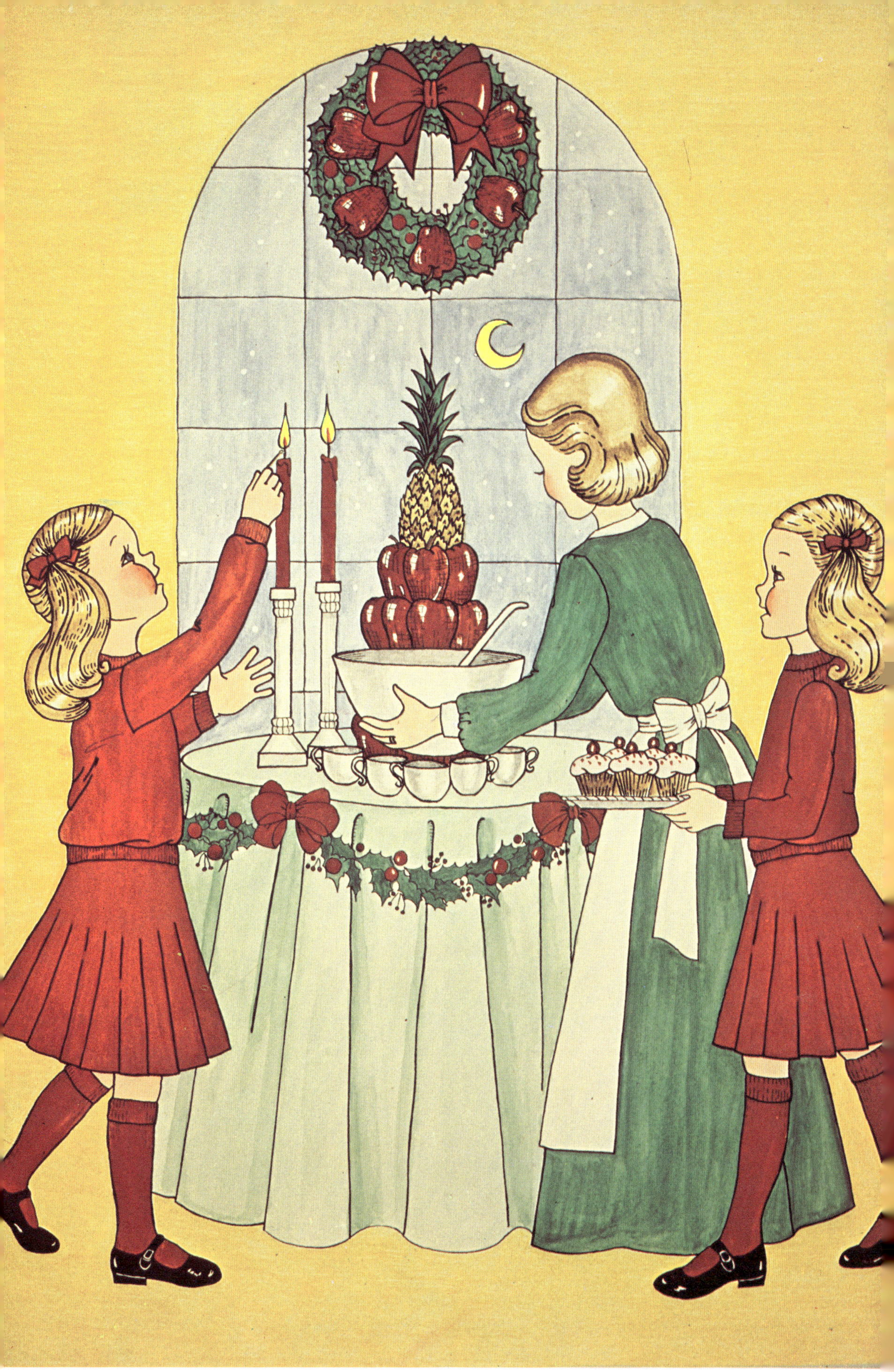

Dr. Wellington began the tree-trimming by arranging the strings of multicolored lights all over the tree. Then everyone joined in hanging hundreds of bright and sparkly ornaments and miniature dolls on every branch until the entire tree was completely covered with shimmering beauty.

When every last ornament had been hung, Mrs. Wellington draped the glittery golden tinsel from branch to branch. After she had finished, Dr. Wellington stood back and gave an admiring glance at the tree. He gave a broad smile of approval and announced that he was ready to place Cherubim, the tree-top angel, on the very top of the tree.

"Wendy and Whitney, please get Cherubim," he called in a happy voice.

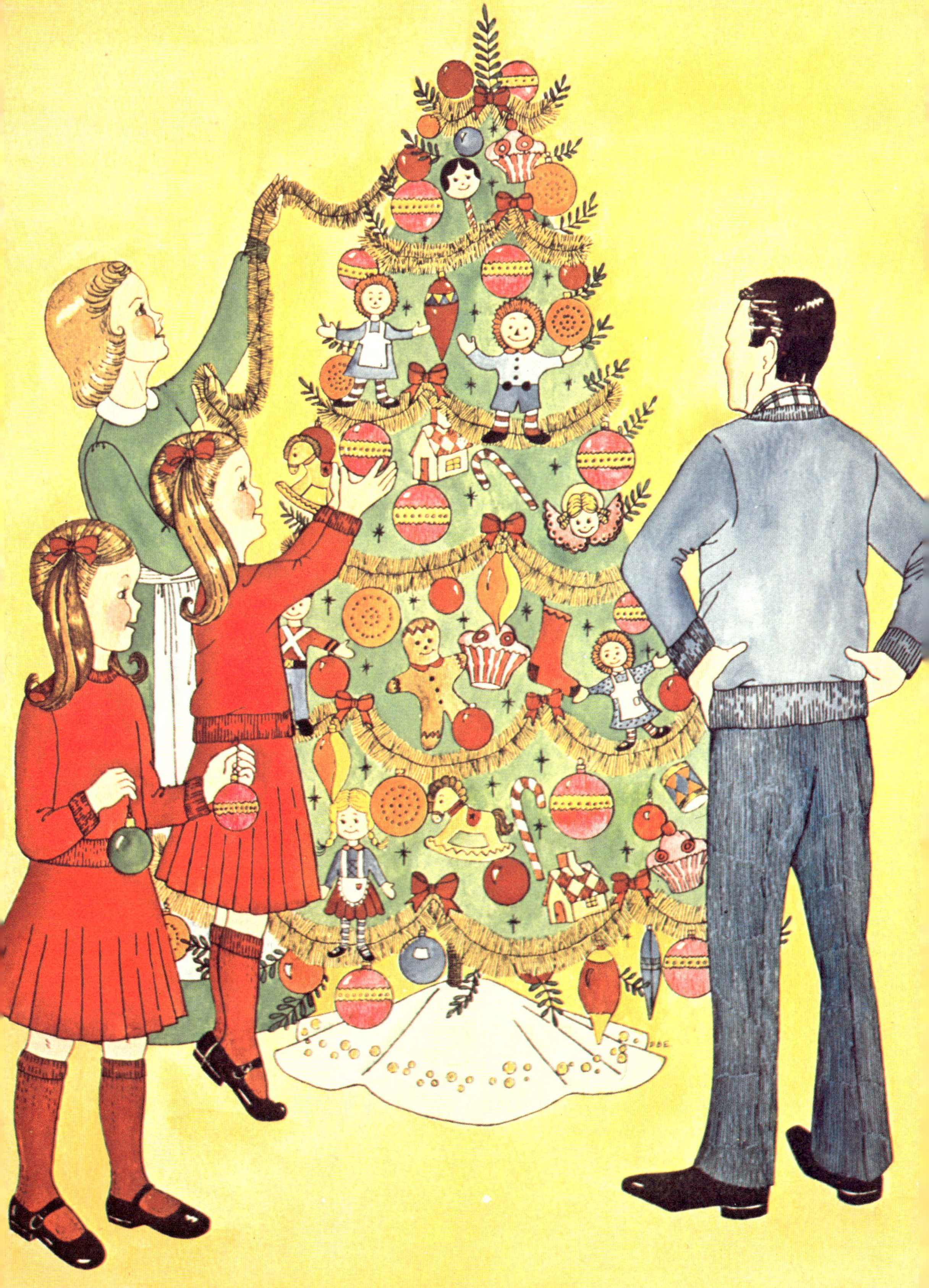

"We're coming, Daddy," chanted the twins in unison, as they scrambled to open the large, well-worn box in which Cherubim had been stored for so many years. They quickly opened it...but to their dismay, the box was empty! Cherubim was not in the box!

Wendy and Whitney looked in every box and carton over and over again, but Cherubim was nowhere to be found!

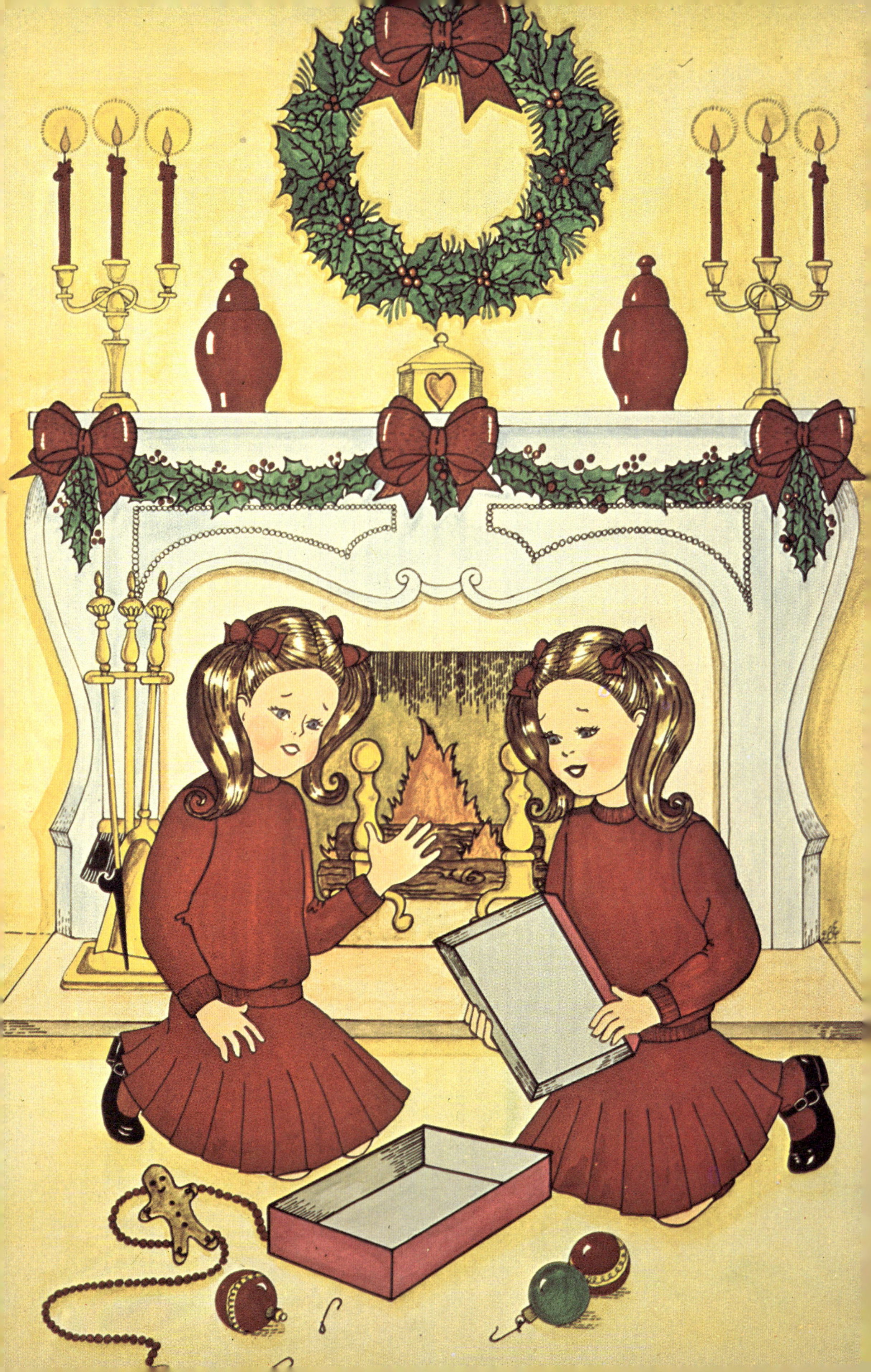

Frantically, the four Wellington children ran back up to the attic. They looked in every box and trunk. They even looked in the drawers of all the old furniture that was stored up there, but there was not a trace of Cherubim anywhere to be found!

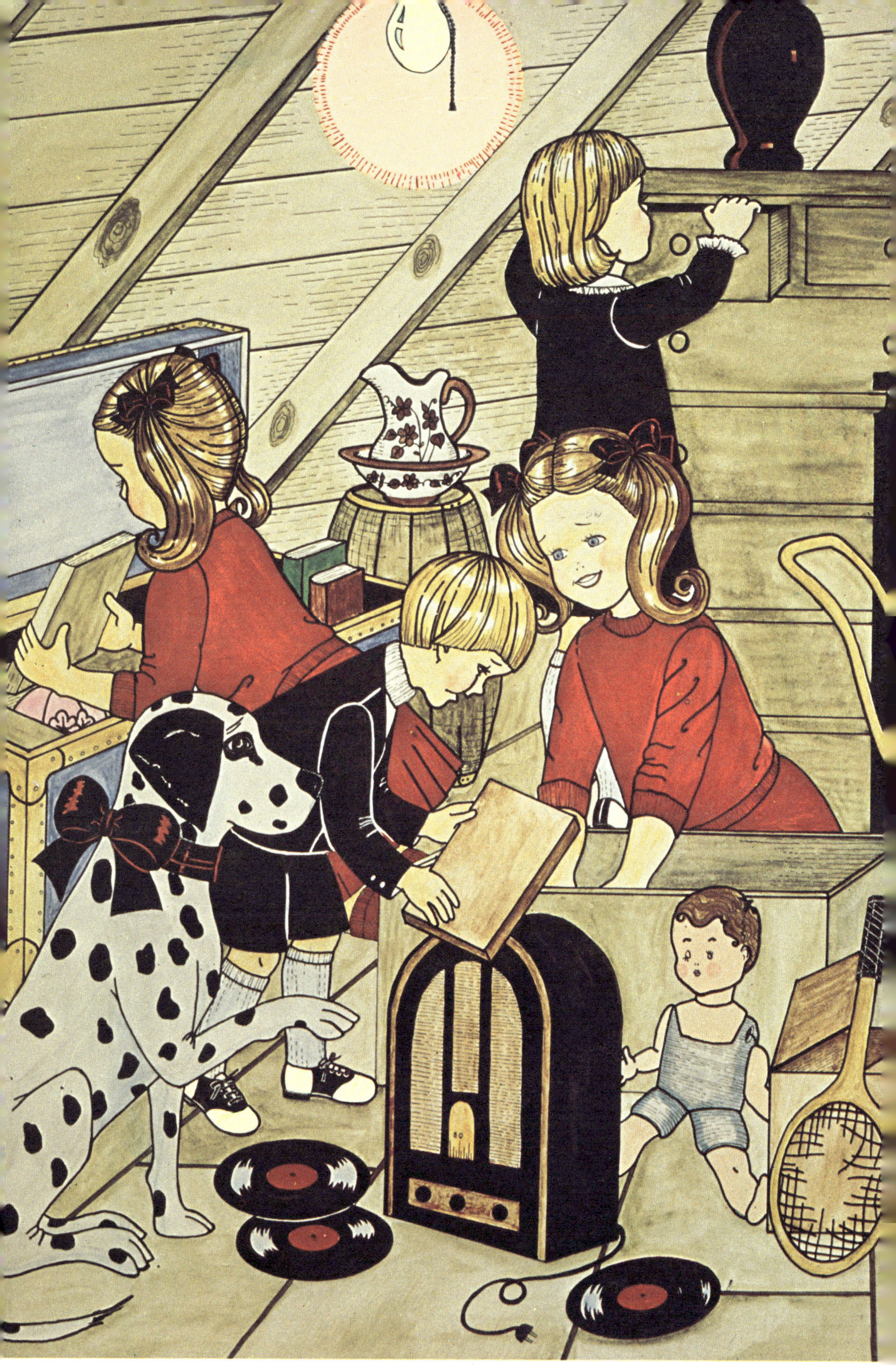

By this time they were all in tears! Mrs. Wellington tried desperately to console them. She dried their tears, put her arms lovingly around them, seated them all beside her on the soft, velvet sofa and began to tell them the story of how Cherubim first came to their family.

"Once upon a time," began Mrs. Wellington, "on one Christmas many, many years ago, when your great, great, great grandmother Bridget Wellington was just a little child like you, she was visiting her Uncle Thomas at his beautiful home, Wellington Castle, in Ireland. In the great hall of the castle stood his tall and magnificent Christmas tree, decorated with hundreds of twinkling candles. On the very top of the tree stood a most beautiful angel, dressed in a dark pink gown, with golden wings and halo. The angel had a very kind and loving face, and Bridget exclaimed to her uncle that it was the most beautiful thing she had ever seen!"

"Did the angel look just like our Cherubim?" asked Patrick, his blue eyes sparkling as he spoke.

"Yes, exactly," said Mrs. Wellington, and she continued on with the story, as she gently tweaked his nose.

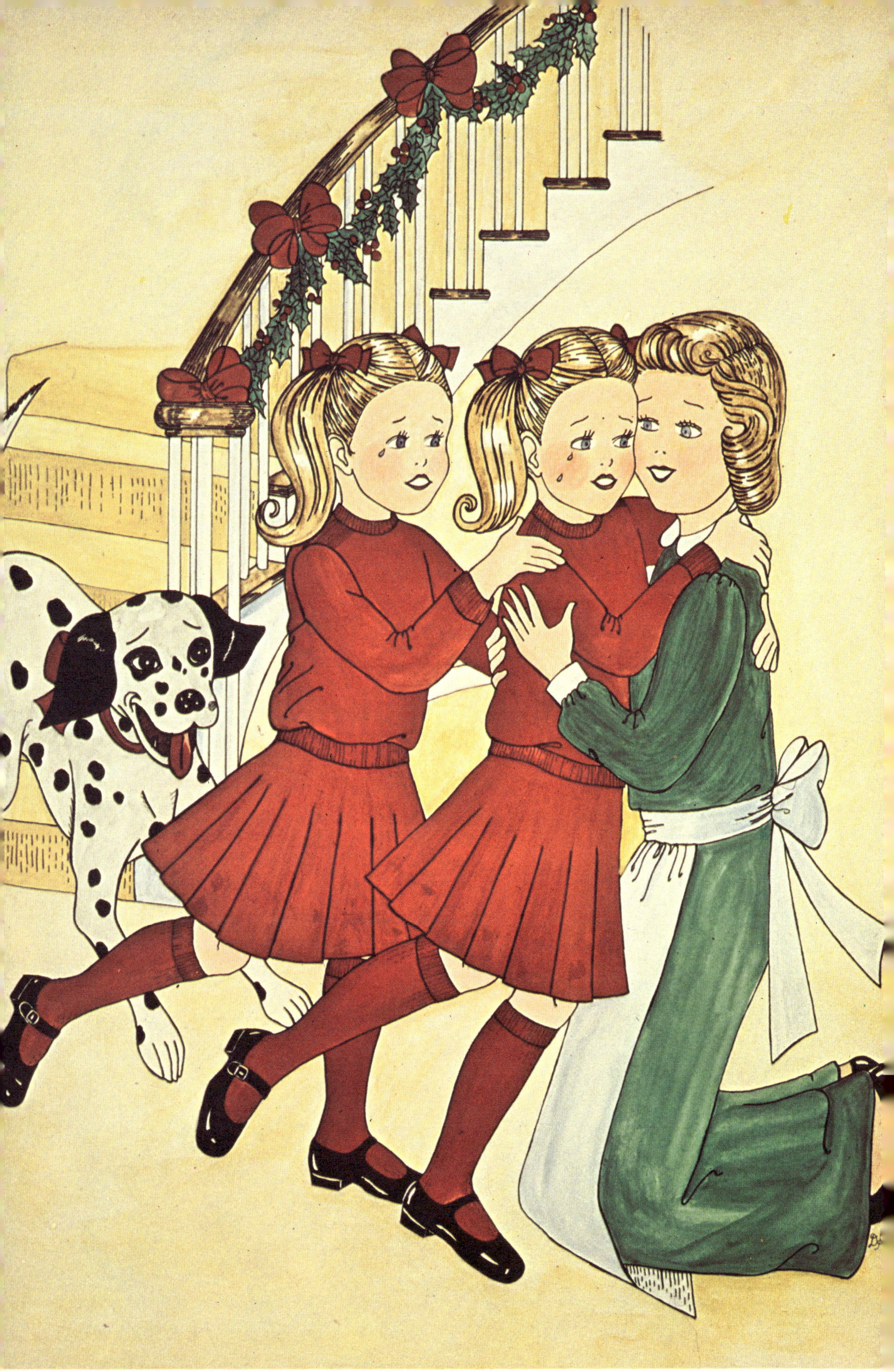

"Uncle Thomas was very touched and reached up to the top of the tree and took the lovely angel down. He placed the angel in Bridget's hands. He told Bridget that early that morning he had seen her give some bread and milk to a poor man who had come to the castle to beg for food. And because of her kindness he wanted her to have the angel. Uncle Thomas told Bridget that the angel's name was Cherubim and that Cherubim was the angel of giving. He warned her that Cherubim would disappear if ever the owner became thoughtless of others and thought only of himself or herself.

"Bridget thanked her uncle and promised always to be kind and charitable.

"After a few years Bridget and her family sailed across the Atlantic Ocean to live in America, and Cherubim was handed down from one generation to the next in the Wellington family until finally the beautiful angel came to our very own family.

"And that is the story of Cherubim, my dears," said Mrs. Wellington. "We will all continue to search for Cherubim, and I feel very confident that we will find our angel before very long. So, please cheer up, my darlings, and don't be sad."

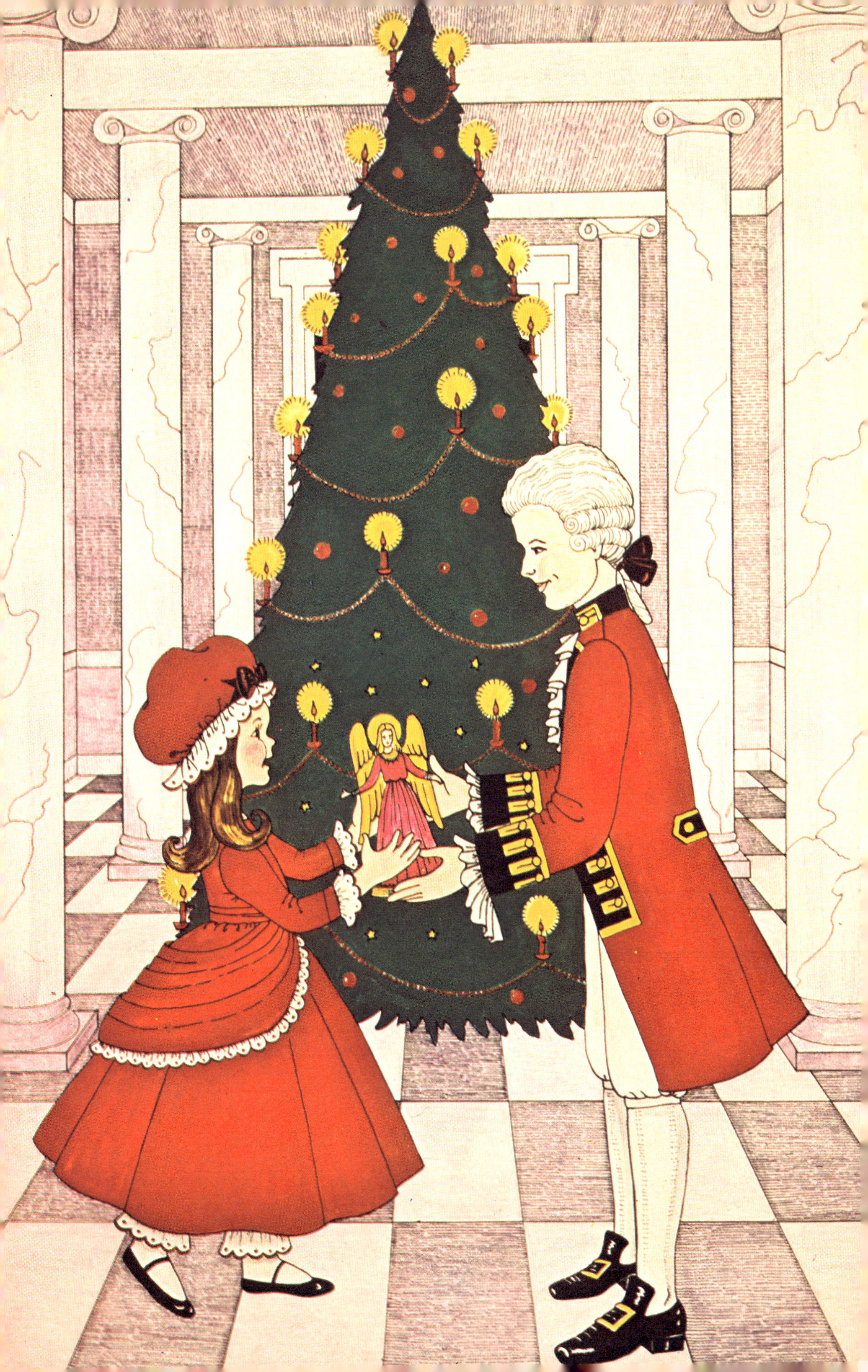

"We'll never find Cherubim!" sobbed Whitney.

"Oh, yes, we will!" answered Wendy confidently. "Now please stop crying, Whitney, and listen to my plan," she pleaded. "I think I know why Cherubim disappeared. It's just like in Mommy's story, when Uncle Thomas told Bridget that Cherubim would disappear if ever the owners became thoughtless of others and thought only of themselves. And that is exactly what has happened to us! We have been thinking only of what we want for Christmas. But now we must start thinking of ways to help others. We must start right now with helping our own family, and then find others who may need our help, and help them! And maybe if we are very helpful and giving, then maybe Cherubim will come back to us!"

"Oh, that's a fairy tale," sobbed Whitney, wiping away a tear which had run down her cheek. "Cherubim was probably thrown out by mistake last Christmas, with some old wrappings and boxes. We'll never find Cherubim no matter what we do!"

"Oh, yes, we will!" exclaimed Wendy with the greatest confidence. "Now, let's go out to the kitchen to help Molly with the dishes, and after we finish, we'll help Mommy and Daddy carry all the empty decoration boxes back up to the attic; and tomorrow we'll help Molly with her long list of Christmas housecleaning chores, which she must finish before Christmas."

"My favorite television program is coming on now. I'll help later," promised Whitney.

"You must come right now, if we ever expect Cherubim to return," commanded Wendy with a grin, as she took Whitney's hand and led her into the kitchen.

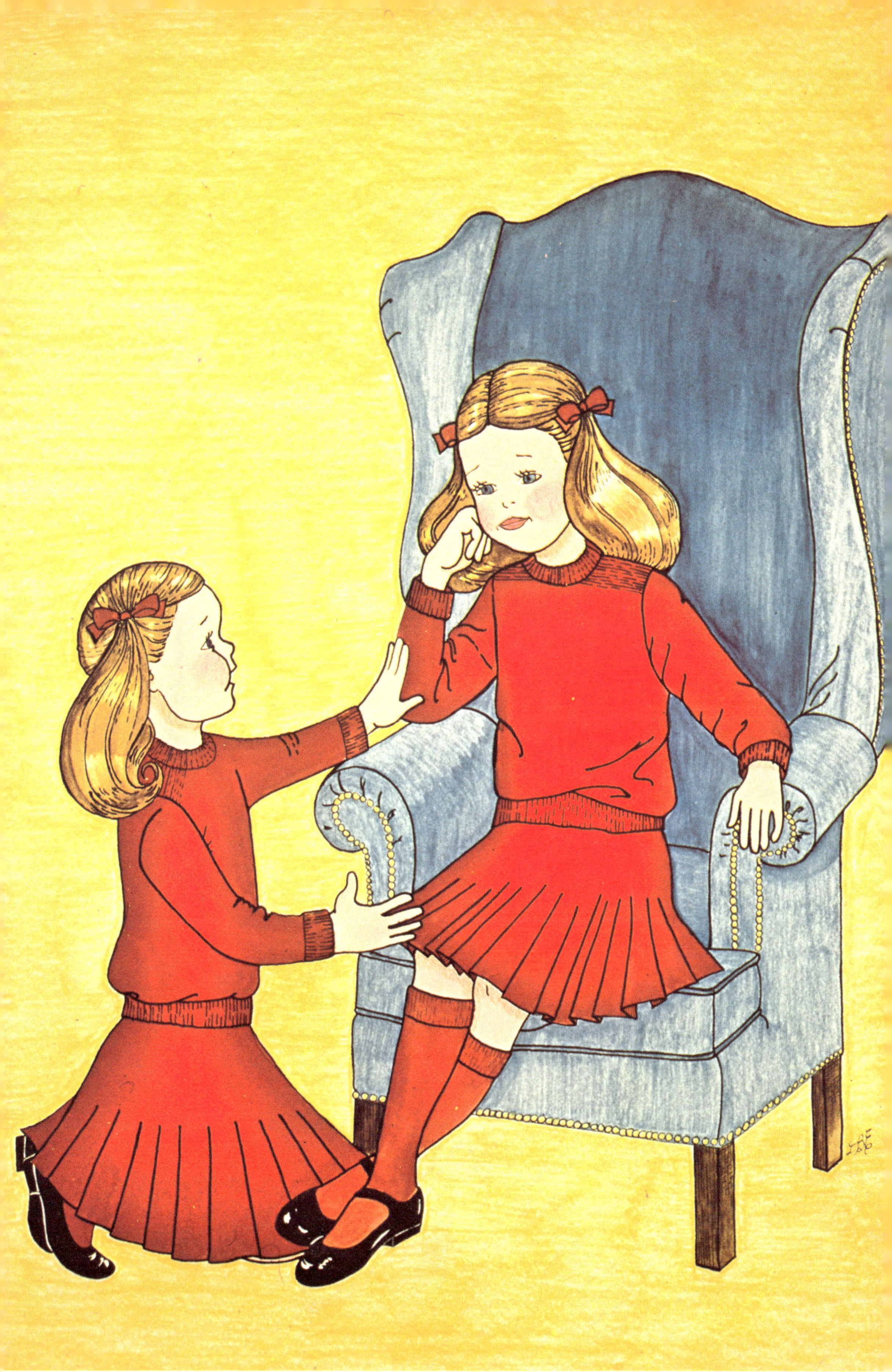

The very next morning Wendy was up bright and early. She was awakened by the merry clinking of dishes and the delicious fragrance of bacon frying. For Molly was already busy in the kitchen.

"Come on, Whitney. It's time to get up," Wendy called, as she gently shook her twin sister.

"It's too early!" complained Whitney, hiding her head under the warm, fluffy quilt.

"We must start early to help Molly with her Christmas housecleaning list," urged Wendy.

Whitney yawned and rubbed her eyes. "All right! All right! I'm coming!" she groaned as she rolled out of bed and walked slowly into the bathroom to dress.

The twins made up their bed and hurried downstairs to the kitchen. After a hearty breakfast they helped Molly with the dishes. Then Wendy went into the living room to vacuum the rugs and dust and polish the furniture.

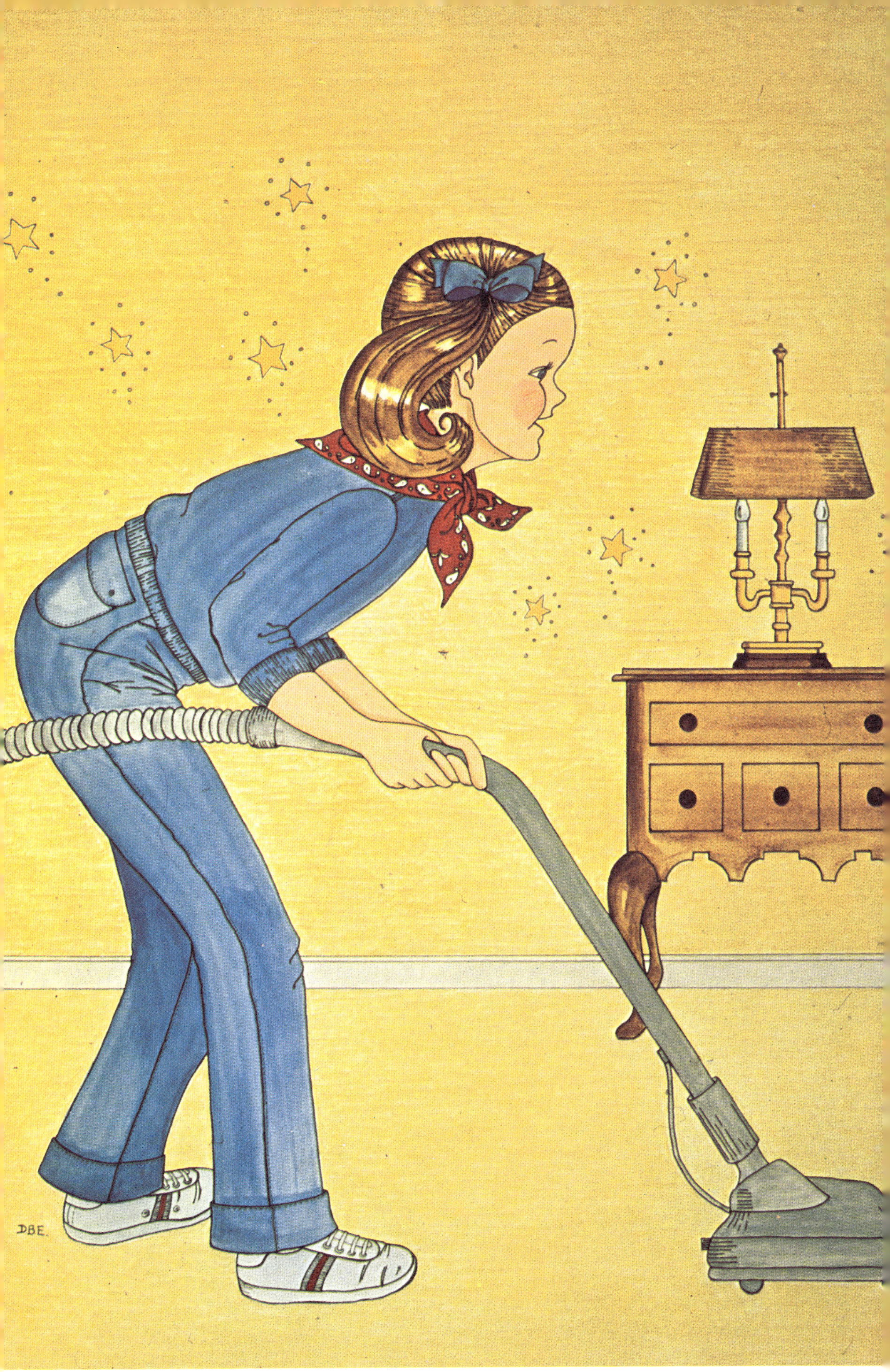
DBE.

Whitney went into the kitchen to scrub the floor, after a little coaxing from Wendy. Then she emptied all the wastebaskets and took out the garbage. The more work she did, the happier she became. She felt so good about herself, she began to hum as she cleaned the bathroom sinks and polished the mirrors. "Maybe Wendy is right," she thought to herself. "Maybe we will find Cherubim if we continue to be helpful and do kind acts."
    From that moment on, Whitney was the first one to volunteer to help, and Wendy never again had to coax her or ask for her help!

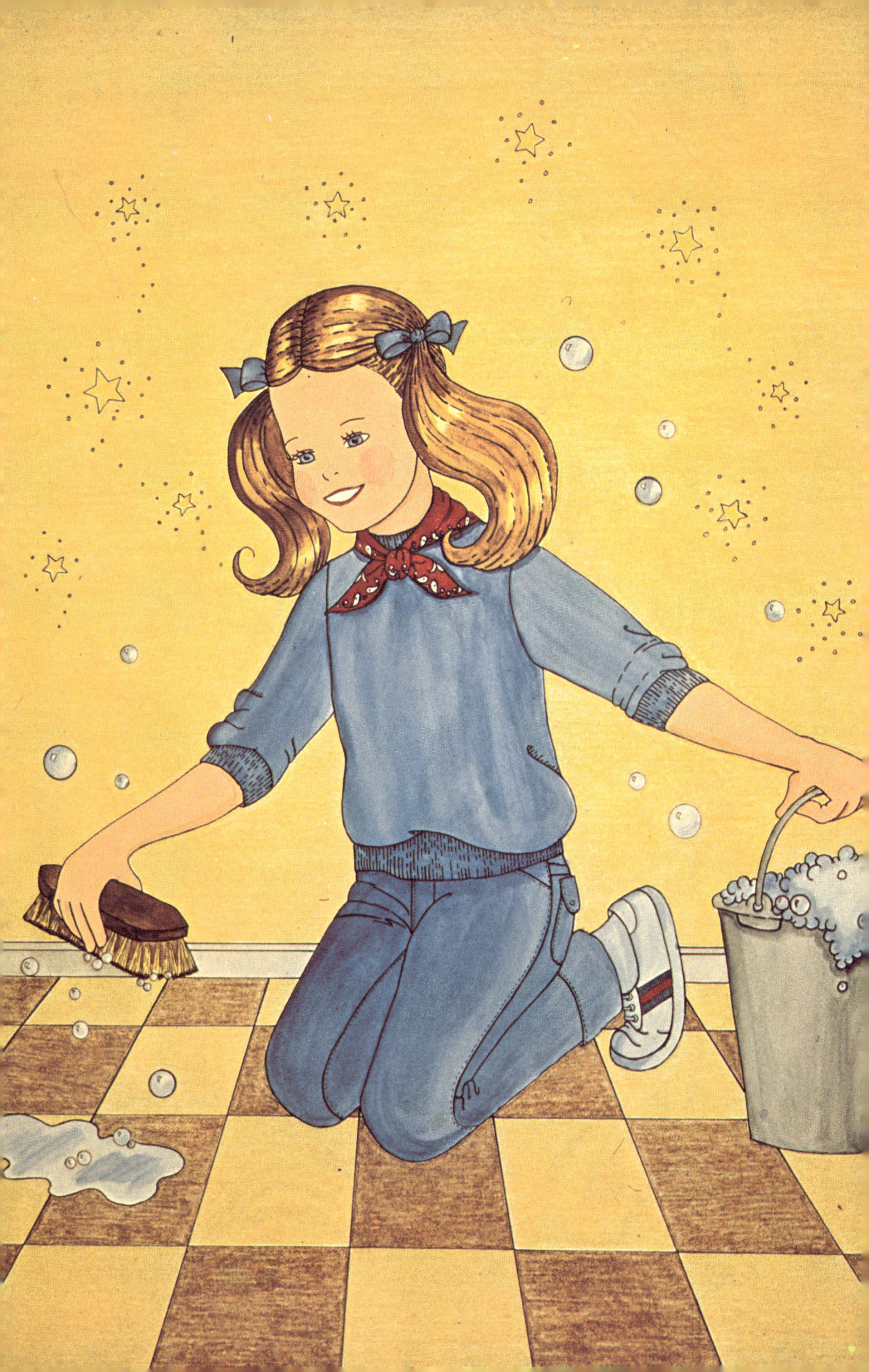

Some days they helped Molly prepare dinner, while Mrs. Wellington went shopping or wrote Christmas cards.

At school, Wendy and Whitney cheered and consoled their classmates who were being hurt or mistreated. They made them feel wanted and loved.

They brought brightly-wrapped Christmas gifts to the children who had to spend Christmas in the hospital.

They entertained at The Home for the Aged, and made the elderly people happy with their Christmas carols.

Despite all their good works, Cherubim still had not returned! Each morning when they awoke, Wendy and Whitney would run into the living room to see if Cherubim was atop the tree—but, alas, Cherubim was not there! They were disappointed, but they would not give up hope.

One bright and sunny morning Mrs. Wellington suggested that Wendy and Whitney accompany her downtown to finish their Christmas shopping.

After a short ride on the train they arrived at downtown Chicago. They walked to State Street, where there are many wonderful stores and shops.

They bought presents for Daddy, Mommy, Patrick, Penny and Molly. And for Spot they bought a huge candy bone!

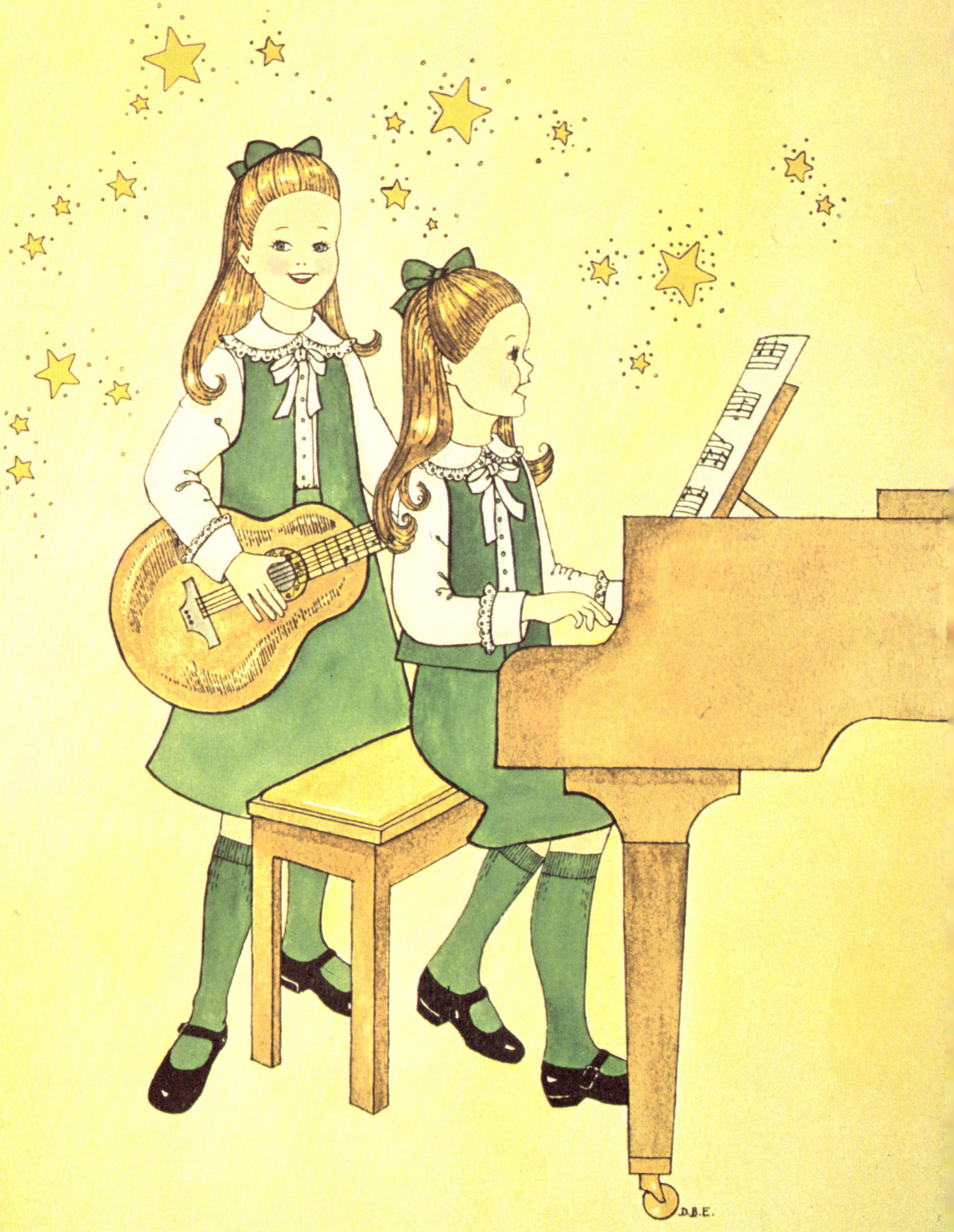
D.B.E.

After a "scrumptious" lunch beneath the exquisitely-decorated Christmas tree at Marshall Fields department store, they visited Santa. He was seated on a large, red velvet chair, surrounded by every toy imaginable. When it was Wendy and Whitney's turn to talk to him, he sat one of them upon each knee. He listened very carefully as the twins told him that all they wanted for Christmas was to have their lost tree-top angel come back to them.

Santa's eyes became very serious as he explained to them that he would do his very best to search for Cherubim, but he could not promise that he would be able to help them, because lost angels are very hard to locate.

Their hearts were very sad, but they still had hopes that Cherubim would return, and they thanked Santa for his help.

Wendy and Whitney were quite tired after shopping most of the day and were relieved and happy when Mommy suggested that they return home, where Molly would have dinner ready and waiting for them.

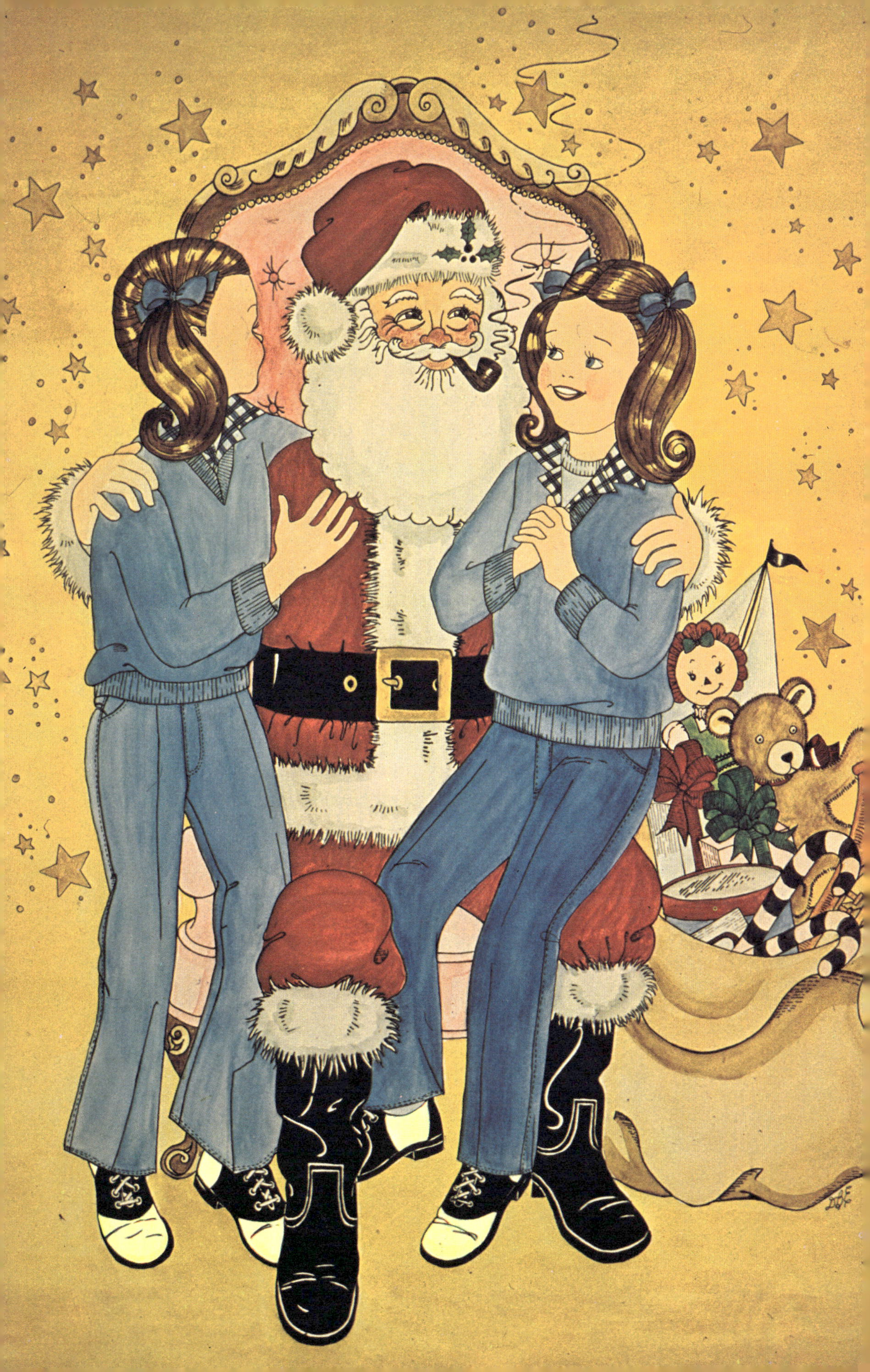

It seemed as if Christmas would never come! The days dragged slowly by until Christmas Eve finally arrived.

Happy and excited laughter filled the kitchen as Wendy and Whitney helped Mrs. Wellington and Molly prepare a special Christmas Eve dinner.

Whitney peeled the potatoes and Wendy made a special jello mold, while Molly made their favorite popovers.

With the dinner in the oven, the twins assisted Mommy in spreading the bright, red tablecloth on the long dining room table. They used the finest china and silver to set the table.

Mrs. Wellington lit the tall, red candles in the silver candelabra, and placed a scarlet poinsettia plant in the center of the table.

Reflections from the crystal chandelier sparkled and danced about the room, as the Wellington family enjoyed the special Christmas Eve dinner of roast beef and popovers.

It was truly a magical night, and excitement mounted.

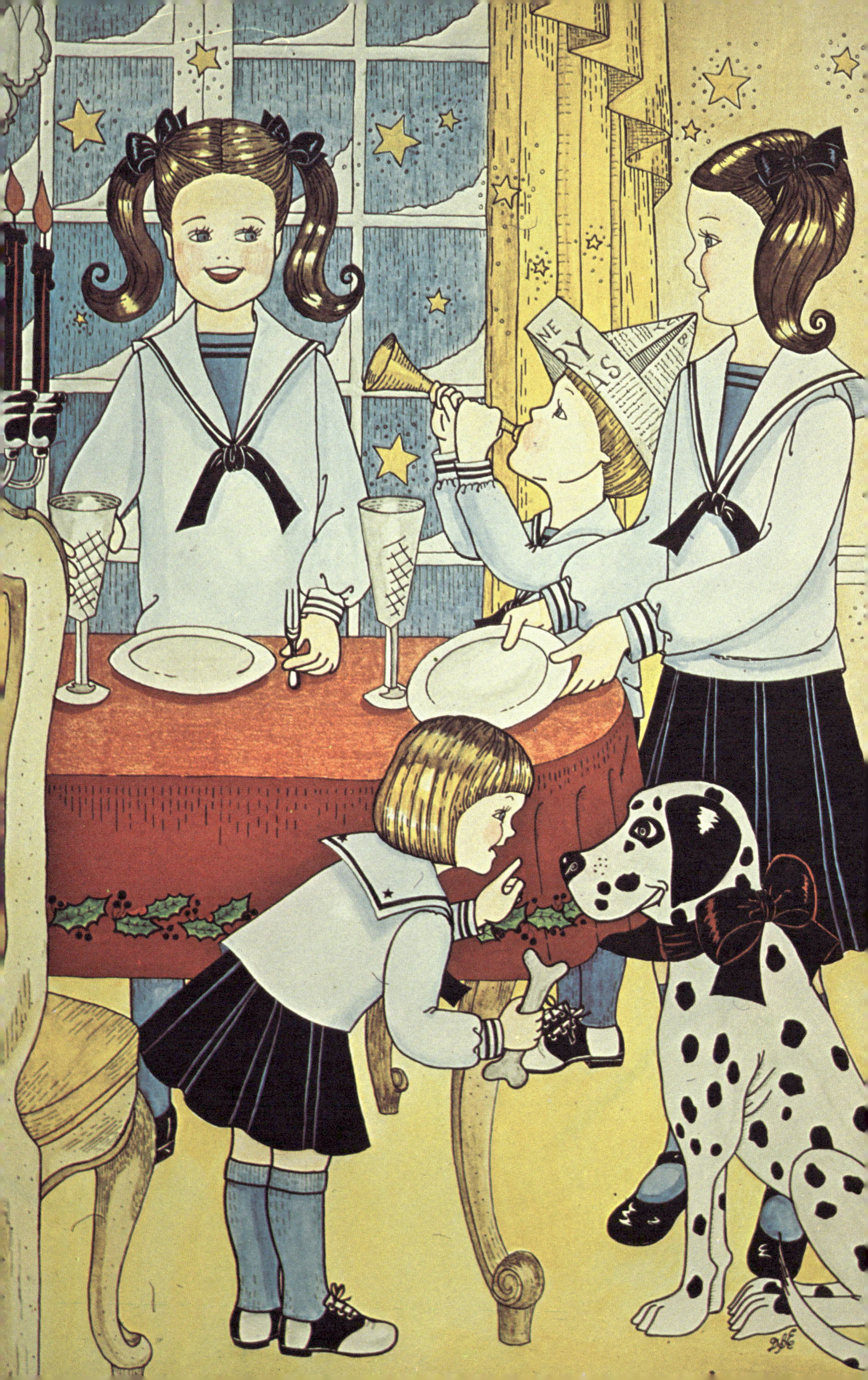

After dinner, while Dr. and Mrs. Wellington wrapped the very last of the Christmas presents, Wendy and Whitney helped Molly straighten the kitchen. When they had finished, they gathered Patrick and Penny into the living room, and on the soft sofa, by the crackling fire, read to them the wondrous story of the first Christmas. It was the beautiful story of the Christ Child, who was born in a stable, nearly two thousand years ago in Bethlehem. "And there were in the field nearby shepherds keeping watch over their flock by night. And the angel of the Lord came upon them, and the glory of the Lord shone round about them, and they were afraid. And the angel said to them, 'Fear not, for I bring you good tidings of great joy, which shall be for all the people. For to you is born this day in the city of David a Savior, Christ the Lord. And this shall be a sign to you: You shall find the infant wrapped in swaddling clothes, lying in a manger.' And suddenly there was with the angel a multitude of the heavenly host praising God, and saying, 'Glory to God in the highest, and on earth peace, good will toward men.'"

Spot sat beside them and listened with great interest, as if he understood every word of the miraculous story.

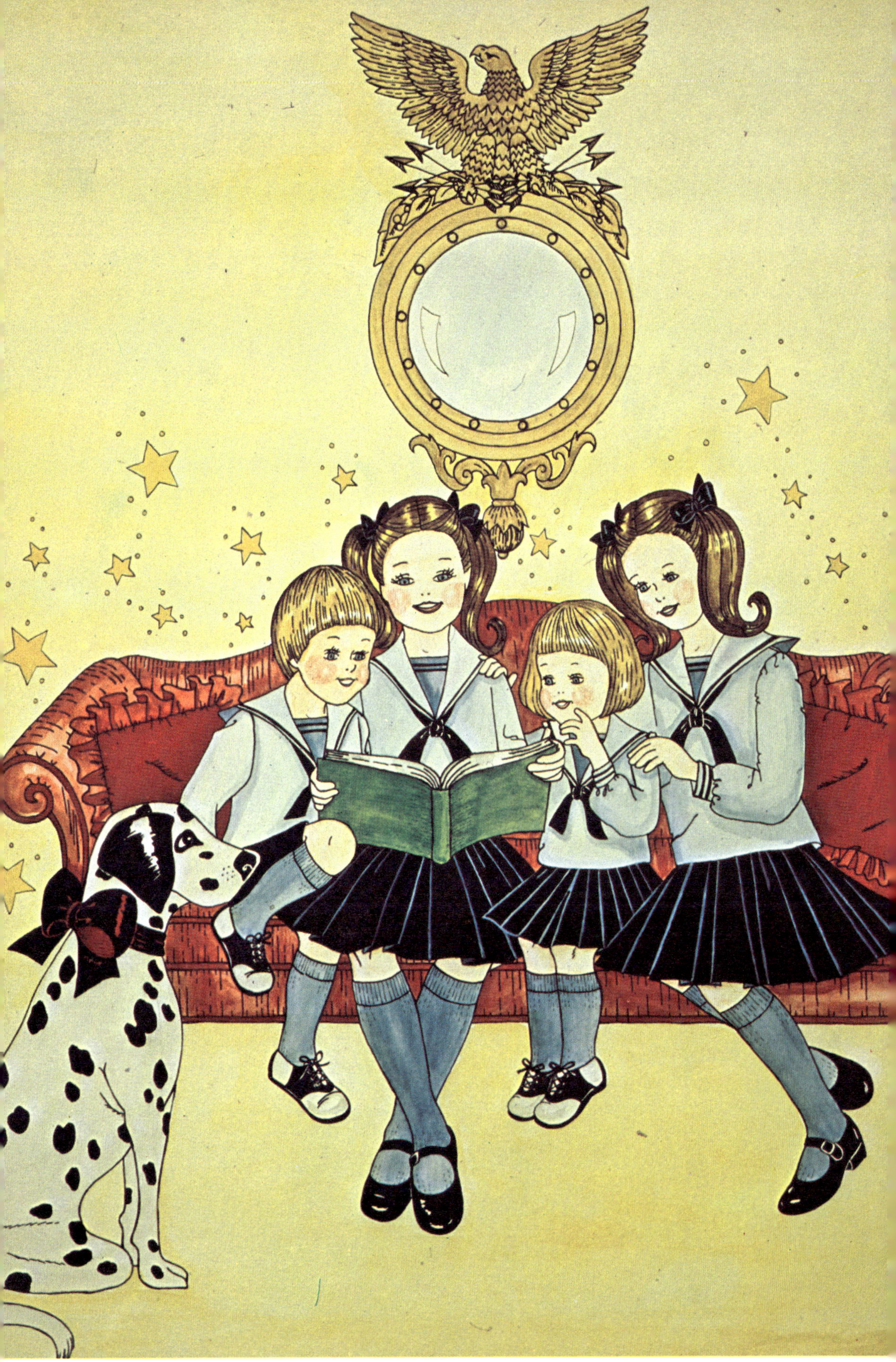

"Time for bed," called Mrs. Wellington, and she and
Dr. Wellington kissed the children good night before they made
their way up the winding staircase to their rooms.

Before retiring, Wendy and Whitney knelt beside their bed
to say their evening prayers. They ended their prayers with
this one:

"Dear God, please bless Mommy and Daddy, Patrick and Penny,
Molly and Spot, and bless all our friends and relatives, too.
And, dear God, please bring Cherubim back to us, if we have been
good enough and are deserving. Thank You, dear God. Amen."

Then they climbed into their big, cozy bed and were soon
off to the land of Christmas dreams.

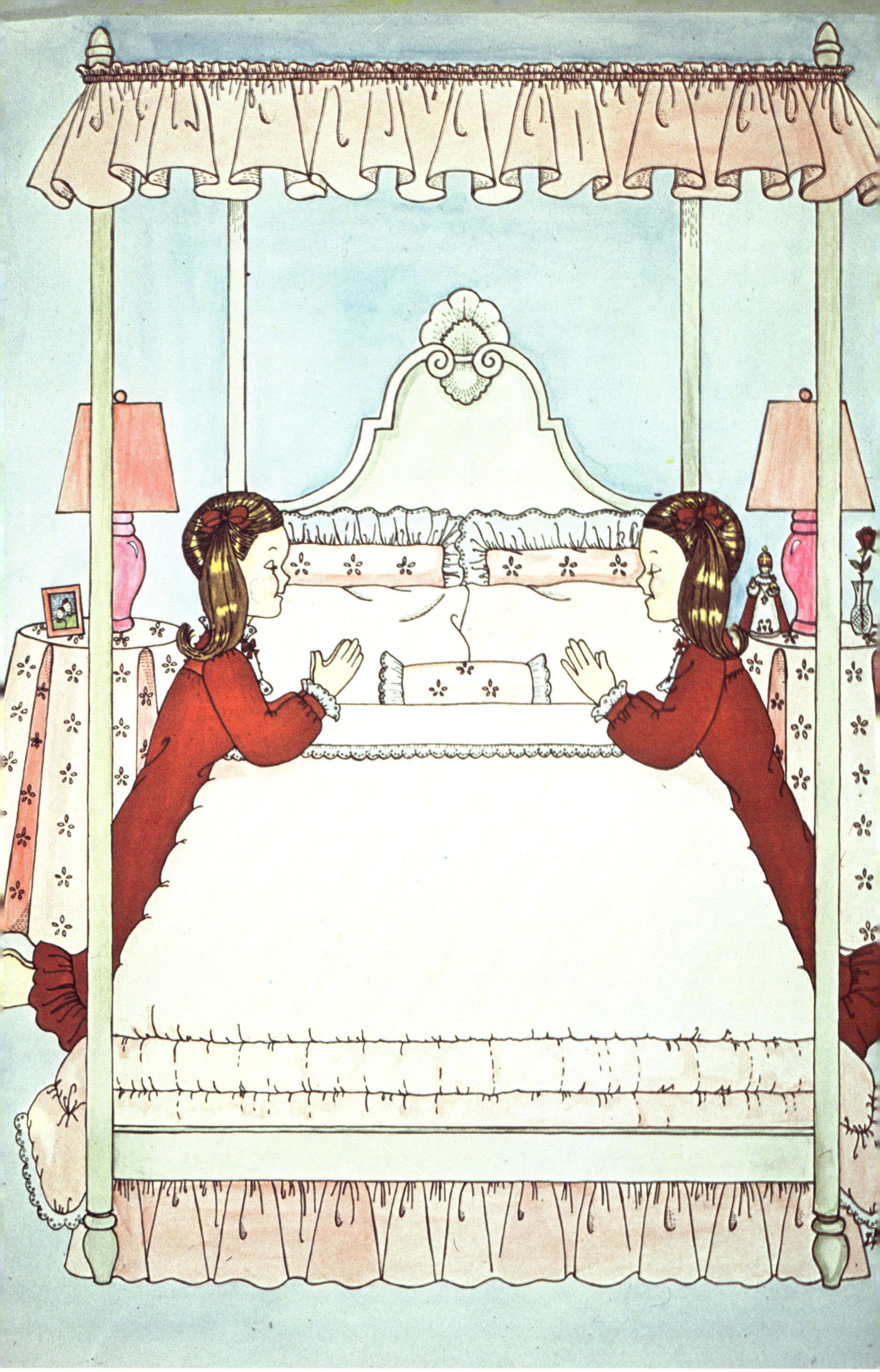

It was just midnight when Wendy and Whitney were awakened by the chiming of the grandfather clock in the front hall. Their room was suddenly filled with a bright light, and a beautiful angel, who looked like a life-sized Cherubim, was bending over their bed.

"Who are you?" asked Wendy, in a trembling voice.

"I am Cherubim, the angel of giving," answered the angel. As Cherubim spoke, hundreds of golden stars twinkled and danced about the room.

"You had always been good and kind girls," said Cherubim softly. "But early in December you were caught up with the festivities of Christmas and were thinking only of yourselves and what you wanted for Christmas. That is why your tree-top angel disappeared. You forgot the true meaning of Christmas, which is helping and giving to others. But in the past two weeks you have done so many good deeds that I have brought you a special surprise for Christmas morning!"

"Oh, thank you!" the twins said politely, their hearts beating wildly.

"These golden stars which you see twinkling about me are the stars of kindness and giving," said Cherubim. "They always appear about someone who performs a kind deed. Only angels can see them, but you can feel them, for they are the happiness you feel inside when you have done something kind. There is more joy in giving than receiving, and it is in giving that we receive." Cherubim concluded by saying: "Merry Christmas, dear children!" and disappeared in a shower of twinkling, golden stars!

Wendy and Whitney rubbed their eyes. Had they been dreaming, or had Cherubim really been there? They would never know for sure, but if it was only a dream, what a wonderful dream it was. And they fell back into a happy Christmas sleep!

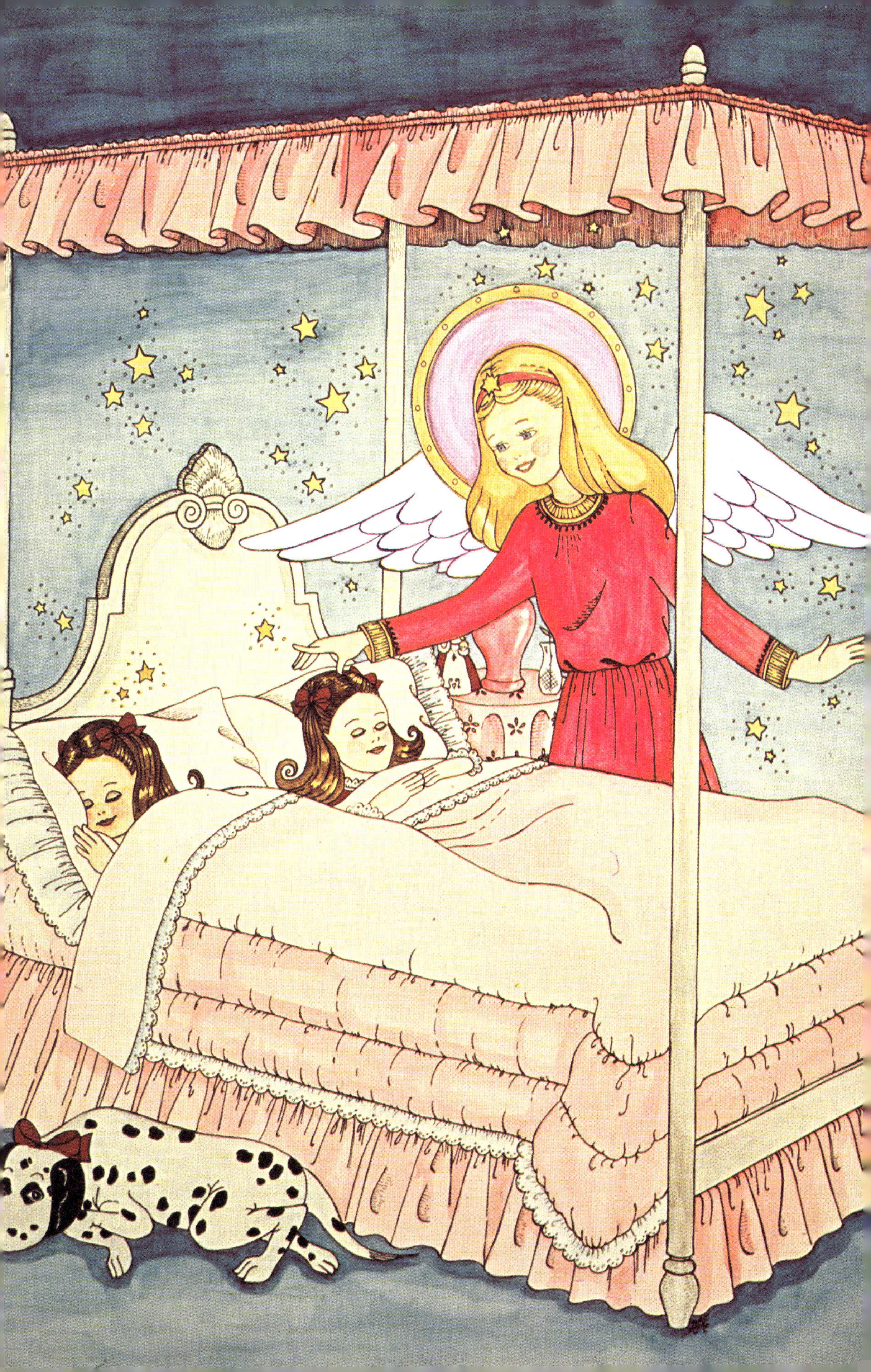

The bright winter sun streamed through the bedroom window, awakening Wendy and Whitney. Christmas was here at last! They pulled on their slippers, called to Patrick and Penny and sped down the staircase, shouting "MERRY CHRISTMAS" at the top of their voices!

They came to a screeching halt as they approached the closed doors to the living room. They stood there for a moment trembling, then they slowly turned the doorknob and peeked in!

They threw open the doors! Lo and behold, there was Cherubim, standing atop the Christmas tree and smiling down at them.

The children gave a rousing cheer!

Even Spot, looking up at Cherubim, seemed to smile, his long curving tail wagging happily.

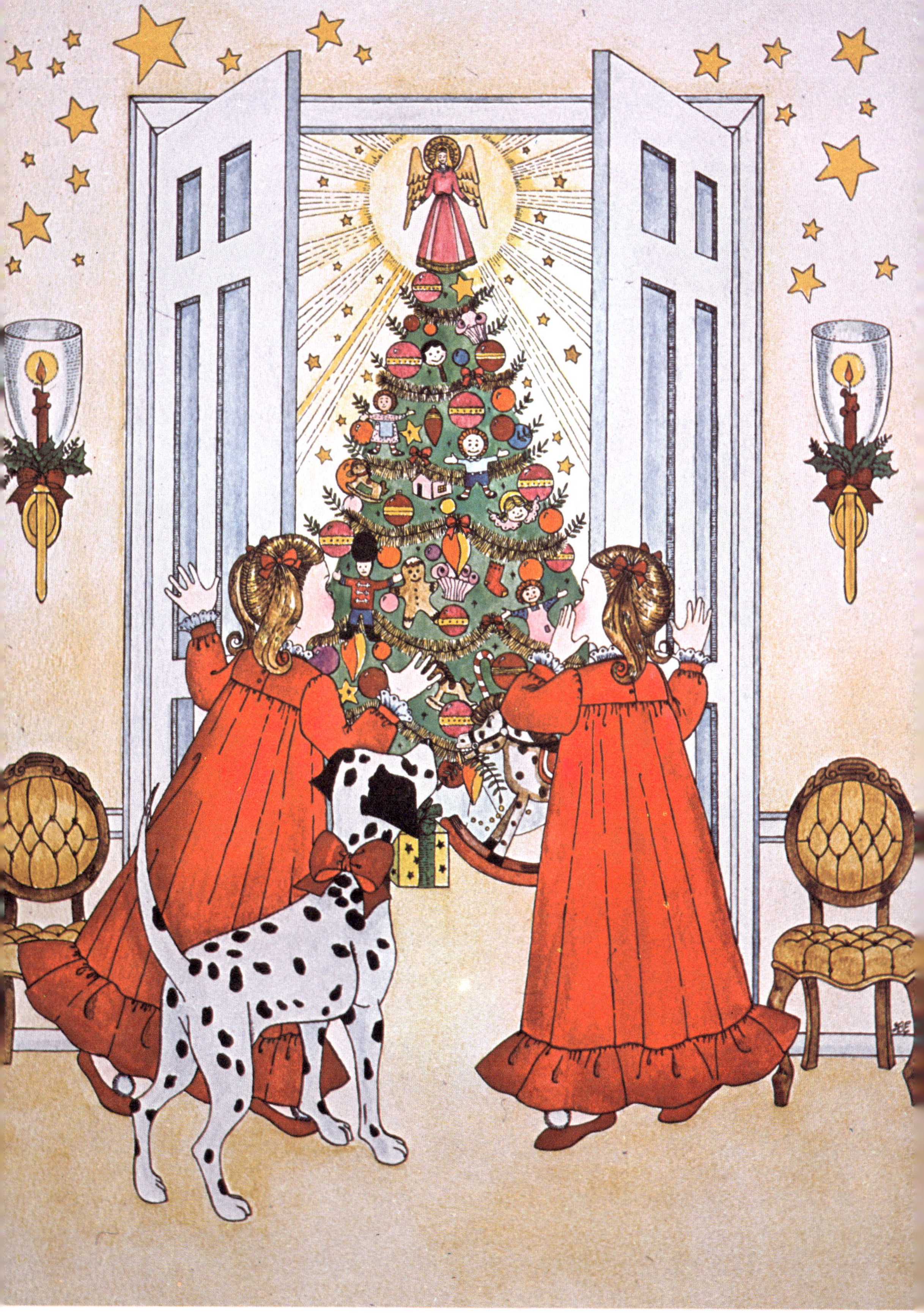

They were filled with such happiness at having Cherubim back that they promised to continue their good works every day of the year and not just at Christmas time.

They were happier than they had ever been before, and that was because they had found more joy in giving than in receiving.

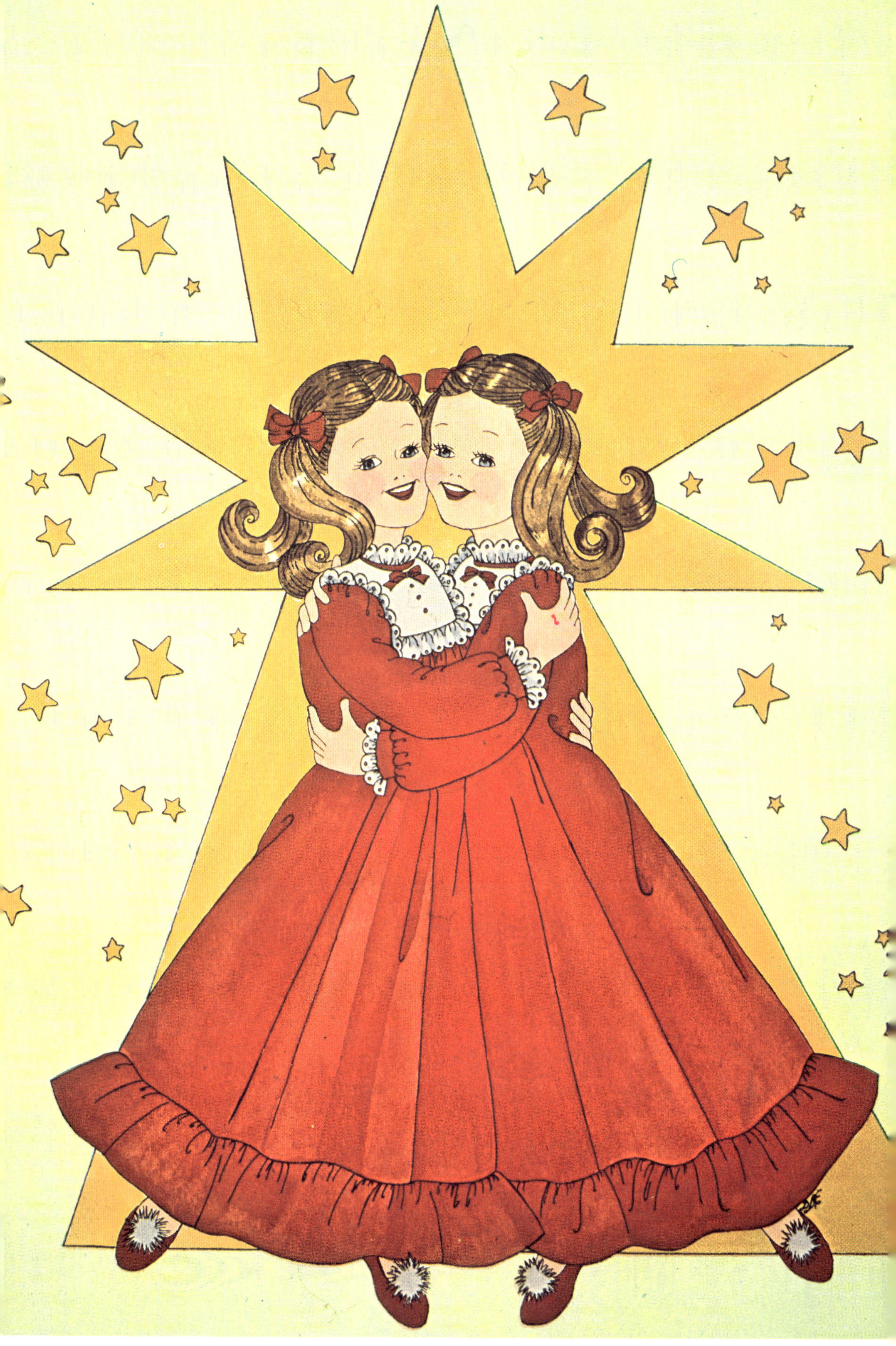

The Wellington family all went to church together on Christmas morning, just as they did every Sunday morning. The wonderful scent of pine, mingled with the fragrance of candles, filled the church. The altar was ablaze with hundreds of poinsettia plants, and the glorious sounds of Christmas music flowed from the magnificent church organ.

Wendy and Whitney bowed their heads in prayer, and lifted their hearts in praise and thanks to Almighty God for all the wonderful blessings He had bestowed upon them and their family, and most especially for having given Cherubim back to them on this happy and holy Christmas morning, and for having made them realize that the true spirit of Christmas is giving.

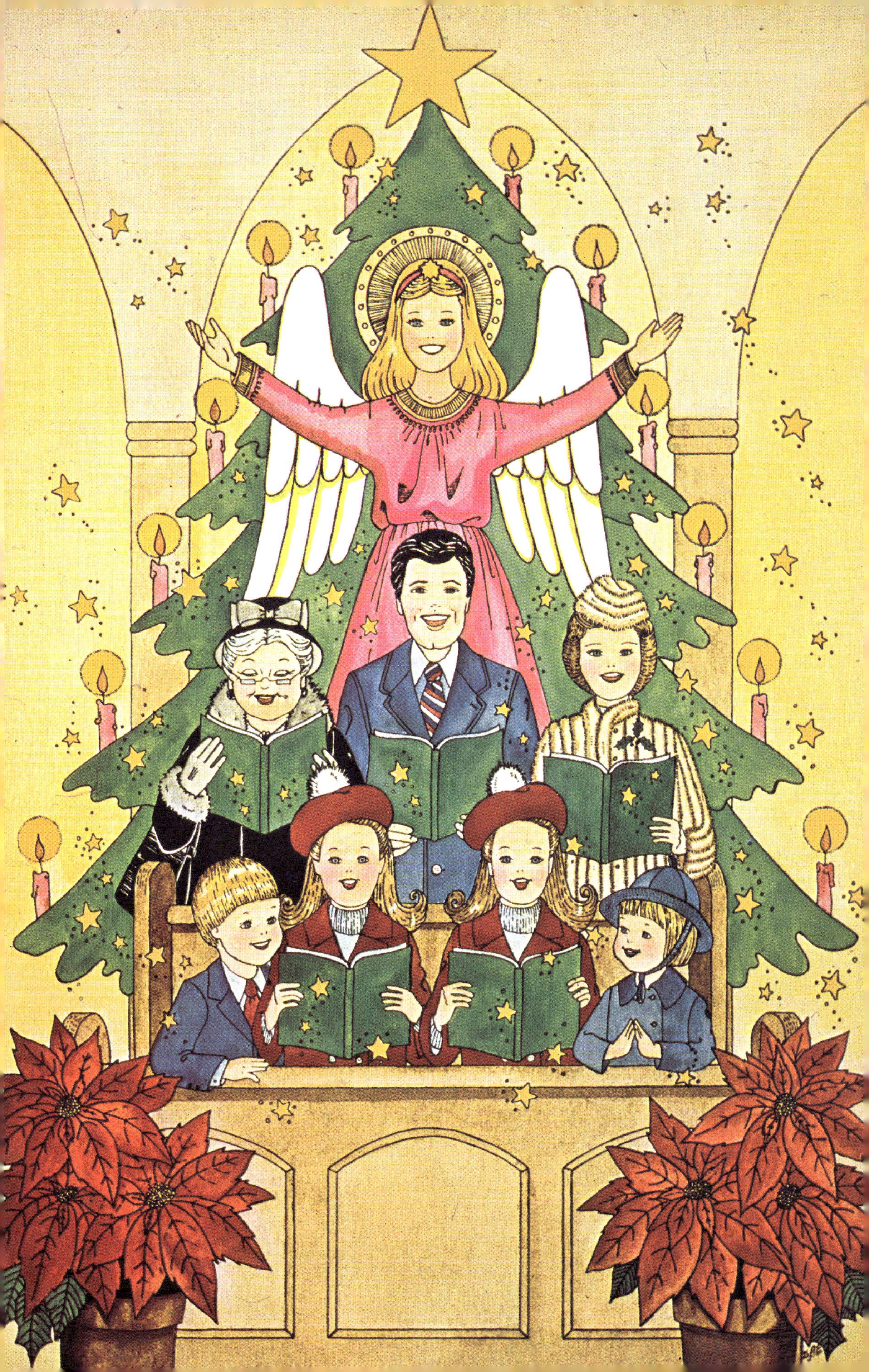

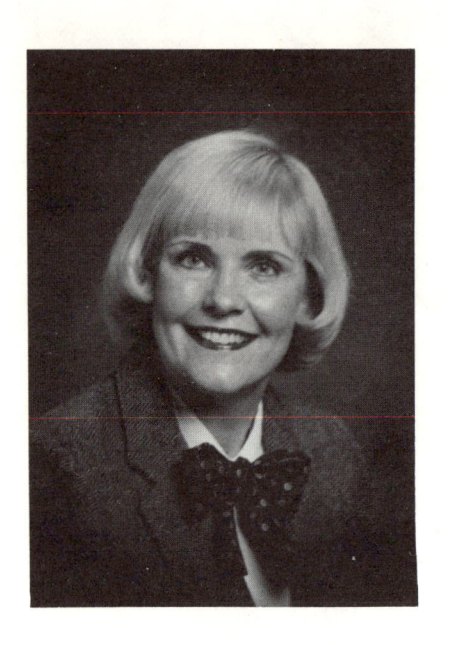

About the Author...

Dolly Biehl Evans, a college graduate, is married to Dr. Thomas Evans, a surgeon. They live in a suburb of Chicago and have four children.

Cherubim is Mrs. Evans' first book. The idea for the story began to evolve a few years ago, when the Evans family lost its own treetop angel.

Wendy and Whitney's Favorite Cookies
DREAM COOKIES

2 egg whites

pinch of salt

¼ tsp. cream of tartar

⅔ cup sugar

1 tsp. vanilla

¼ tsp. almond flavor

1 cup chopped pecans

¾ cup chocolate chips

Preheat oven to 350°. Beat egg whites until foamy. Add salt and cream of tartar and continue to beat until stiff. Very gradually add sugar, then vanilla and almond extract. Peaks should be shiny and stiff. Fold in nuts and chocolate chips. Drop by teaspoon onto greased cookie sheet. Place in oven. Turn oven off. Leave cookies in the oven until morning. No peeking or you will lose oven heat.

Daughters of St. Paul

IN MASSACHUSETTS
 50 St. Paul's Ave., Jamaica Plain, Boston, MA 02130; **617-522-8911.**
 172 Tremont Street, Boston, MA 02111; **617-426-5464; 617-426-4230.**

IN NEW YORK
 78 Fort Place, Staten Island, NY 10301; **212-447-5071; 212-447-5086.**
 59 East 43rd Street, New York, NY 10017; **212-986-7580.**
 625 East 187th Street, Bronx, NY 10458; **212-584-0440.**
 525 Main Street, Buffalo, NY 14203; **716-847-6044.**

IN NEW JERSEY
 Hudson Mall—Route 440 and Communipaw Ave.,
  Jersey City, NJ 07304; **201-433-7740.**

IN CONNECTICUT
 202 Fairfield Ave., Bridgeport, CT 06604; **203-335-9913.**

IN OHIO
 2105 Ontario Street (at Prospect Ave.), Cleveland, OH 44115; **216-621-9427.**
 25 E. Eighth Street, Cincinnati, OH 45202; **513-721-4838; 513-421-5733.**

IN PENNSYLVANIA
 1719 Chestnut Street, Philadelphia, PA 19103; **215-568-2638.**

IN VIRGINIA
 1025 King Street, Alexandria, VA 22314; **703-683-1741; 703-549-3806.**

IN FLORIDA
 2700 Biscayne Blvd., Miami, FL 33137; **305-573-1618.**

IN LOUISIANA
 4403 Veterans Memorial Blvd., Metairie, LA 70002; **504-887-7631; 504-887-0113.**
 1800 South Acadian Thruway, P.O. Box 2028, Baton Rouge, LA 70821; **504-343-4057; 504-381-9485.**

IN MISSOURI
 1001 Pine Street (at North 10th), St. Louis, MO 63101; **314-621-0346; 314-231-1034.**

IN ILLINOIS
 172 North Michigan Ave., Chicago, IL 60601; **312-346-4228; 312-346-3240.**

IN TEXAS
 114 Main Plaza, San Antonio, TX 78205; **512-224-8101; 512-224-0938.**

IN CALIFORNIA
 1570 Fifth Ave., San Diego, CA 92101; **619-232-1442.**
 46 Geary Street, San Francisco, CA 94108; **415-781-5180.**

IN WASHINGTON
 2301 Second Ave., Seattle, WA 98121.

IN HAWAII
 1143 Bishop Street, Honolulu, HI 96813; **808-521-2731.**

IN ALASKA
 750 West 5th Ave., Anchorage, AK 99501; **907-272-8183.**

IN CANADA
 3022 Dufferin Street, Toronto 395, Ontario, Canada.

IN ENGLAND
 199 Kensington High Street, London W8 63A, England.
 133 Corporation Street, Birmingham B4 6PH, England.
 5A-7 Royal Exchange Square, Glasgow G1 3AH, England.
 82 Bold Street, Liverpool L1 4HR, England.

IN AUSTRALIA
 58 Abbotsford Rd., Homebush, N.S.W. 2140, Australia.